Healthful
Simple & Wholesome

My Recipes

And an Array of Desserts

Jean N. Petranto

CONTENTS

1   About The Author   Pg # 1

2   Soups   Pg # 5

3   Pasta   Pg # 15

4   Vegetables   Pg # 29

5   Main Dishes   Pg # 37

6   Desserts   Pg # 51

7   Recipe Index   Pg # 89

JEAN N. PETRANTO

A SUMMARY OF LOVE, LIFE & AMBITION

JEAN N. PETRANTO

First is faith and love for the Lord who makes all things possible. Second is a happy family who benefits from healthful, wholesome foods.

At the age of 89 I wrote my first cookbook, which has sold more than 400 copies to date. I have been approached by friends and readers time and time again to write a second cookbook with an expanded section on cookies and desserts.

Now at 92 I've taken the challenge of putting the recipes from memory down into this new book. It's hard writing since I suffer from macular degeneration, which makes me almost 90% blind. Through the grace of God, keeping close to my writing, I've finally reached my goal of book number two!

This book is dear to my heart. My hope is that it will help families become closer and healthier. Many teenagers do not eat nutritious foods, possibly because it is not available at home. Oftentimes when they become adults they find themselves sick, unhappy, overweight and without ambition.

Too many people find life so hard they turn away from the Lord. Turning instead to drugs, sex and other illusory comforts, which have the result of lessening the possibility of a healthy, happy family life.

It is important to remember that Jesus loves everyone no matter how bad their actions were in the past. If we get on our knees and ask the Lord's forgiveness, his love will change our lives.

When I was seven years old I had no choice but to learn to cook and take care of my brothers and sisters after my mother died. With help from my father, who was a great cook, I persevered and my family thrived.

I can't remember any of us going to the doctor or dentist or ever being sick. We walked two miles back and forth to school and suffered not even a cold.

We ate right! None of us were overweight. All of us worked and helped out. We all had our chores to do. We had a garden with wonderful vegetables – the very best! The biggest tomatoes, peppers, green beans and corn were ours. I learned to make all kinds of soups and stews – mainly Italian dishes.

In 1927 there were no gas ranges. We had a black stove with four burners and coal and wood were our fuel. We had to keep the fire in the stove burning, for if it went out we had no heat!

We rarely ate out and only then with a special invitation. We relished home cooked meals. They made us healthier!

Cooking wholesome foods for us represented love of family…a way to be together, eat together, pray together and maintain strength using kindness and caring.

My motto has been: "Try to achieve all you can." A couch looks good when you are tired, but don't lie down, use your body! Walk, care for your pets, clean the house and garage … circulate the blood that runs through your veins! You'll feel better and your home will be cleaner too!

If I come on strong it is because the world is full of sin and corruption. No one person on earth can change everything. Only you, not politicians or lawyers, and the good Lord who commands all. The secret is not to give up. Be calm, good within your heart and things will fall into place. Try these recipes, they are simple. Keep trying, don't ever give up because food is essential to the body – it's what makes us well!

I take care of my 95 year old husband. We've been married 72 years. I still cook and keep up a large home and entertain family and friends regularly.

I wish you the very best of luck and best wishes for the future. Remember life is what you make it; turn away from evil and turn toward good – all the days of your life.

Good luck, eat well and keep moving. God bless you and yours.

Jean N. Petranto

SOUPS

ZUCCHINI MINESTRA

2 small zucchini, diced
½ head of romaine, chopped fine
2 potatoes, diced
¼ cup pure olive oil
3 stalks celery, chopped
1 onion, chopped
4 cloves garlic, mince
1 14 oz. can or 1 cup fresh tomatoes, chopped
Small pasta such as orzo

Sauté zucchini, celery, onion, garlic and potatoes in olive oil – cook 5 minutes.

Add 1 quart water – salt and pepper (or stock). Cook until tender. Add handful of small pasta, cook about 5 minutes or until pasta is al dente. Sprinkle with Parmesan cheese.

MINESTRONE

½ cup pure olive oil
6 cloves garlic – minced
1 large onion, diced
4 celery stalks, diced
4 fresh tomatoes or 1 large can diced tomatoes
Salt and pepper
1 tsp. basil
sprinkle of oregano
crushed red pepper
2 large potatoes, diced
2 carrots, diced
½ head small cabbage, chopped
1 zucchini, diced
1 can tomato paste
2 cups cannellini or chick peas

In large saucepan heat olive oil. Add garlic, onion and celery, sauté until soft. Add tomatoes, paste, seasonings and 1 quart of water. Bring to a boil, add remaining ingredients. Lower heat and cook until tender.

In another kettle, cook potatoes, carrots and cabbage in salted water until just tender. Add to soup, using some of the water as needed .

Meat Lovers – add 2 links of sliced Italian sausage, removed from casing, or ½ lb. stew beef, browned. Add while soup is cooking.

CAULIFLOWER SOUP

¼ cup pure virgin olive oil
1 head of cauliflower, cut in small pieces
6 cloves of garlic, minced
8 oz. angel hair pasta
Grated Parmesan cheese
Sprinkle of fresh chopped parsley
Salt and pepper to taste

Heat olive oil in large kettle. Sauté chopped cauliflower with garlic for 5 minutes. Cover with water, until pan is 3/4 full, season with salt and pepper and cover. Cook until tender, stirring often.

In food processor, break angel hair pasta into ¼" to ½" pieces. Cook in boiling water for 2-3 minutes. Drain and add to soup.

May add a little pasta water to soup to thin it. Sprinkle with parsley, parmesan cheese, black pepper and parsley.

BEST ONION SOUP

2 large onions, sliced
5 Tbsp. butter, separated
2 Tbsp. pure olive oil
2 ½ Tbsp. flour
4 cups of beef stock (preferably homemade)
2 garlic cloves, minced
Day old Italian or French Bread, cut into large crouton size pieces
½ lb. fresh mozzarella cheese, cut into ½" thick slices
½ lb. grated cheese

Heat butter and oil in skillet sauce pan. Sauté onions until golden brown. Put into a bowl.

In large sauce pan, add beef stock and flour, bring to a boil, stirring until slightly thickened. Season with pepper. Set aside.

Heat remaining butter in skillet, add garlic and bread pieces. stirring until golden brown. Set aside.

Assemble into 4 ceramic bowls:
1 slice mozzarella
Beef Broth
Onions
crushed red pepper if desired
1 slice mozzarella
Bread
1 slice mozzarella
Parmesan cheese

Bake in 350° oven for 30 minutes or until golden brown.

LENTIL SOUP

1 lb. lentils
¼ cup pure olive oil
½ head celery, chopped
1 onion, chopped
4 cloves garlic, minced
1 head of fennel leaves, chopped fine (optional)
1 lb. of fresh or 1 large can of crushed tomatoes
¼ tsp. oregano
2 potatoes, diced
Crushed red pepper
Salt and pepper to taste
Grated Parmesan cheese
Crushed red pepper
Small pasta

Rinse lentils. Pour 4 quarts of water over lentils and cook until slightly tender about 1 hour. Set aside.

In separate saucepan, heat oil. Sauté celery, onions, garlic, fennel (if using) until silvery. Add potatoes, paste and tomatoes. Cook until potatoes are tender.

Add potato mixture to lentils. Add a handful of small soup pasta (if desired) and cook for about 10 minutes longer. Top servings with cheese & crushed red pepper.

CABBAGE MINESTRA (ITALIAN SOUP)

¼ cup pure olive oil
1 head cabbage, shredded
2 potatoes, diced
3 celery stalks, diced
1 large onion, diced
4 cloves garlic, minced
1 can diced tomatoes (1 cup fresh)
1 can chick peas
Salt and pepper
Parmesan cheese
Pasta or rice

In saucepan, heat olive oil. Sauté cabbage, potatoes, celery, onions and garlic. Cook until tender.

Add 1 quart water or homemade chicken stock (good with water). Add tomatoes and chick peas. Reheat over low heat and serve immediately.

Add a handful of small pasta or rice and cook until tender.

FRESH BROCCOLI SOUP

¼ cup pure oil
1 large head of broccoli, cut into small pieces
1 large onion, chopped
6 cloves garlic, minced
½ cup fresh or frozen peas, rinsed (optional)
2 cups rice
Crushed red pepper
¼ cup parsley, chopped
Parmesan cheese

Heat oil. Add broccoli, onions, garlic and sauté for 5 minutes. Cover with water, add salt & pepper or red crushed pepper and cook until tender, about 45 minutes. Add peas if desired.

Cook 2 cups of rice and add to broccoli. Serve with cheese & sprinkle of parsley. If dry, add more water.

BEAN SOUP WITH TOMATOES AND RICE

¼ cup pure olive oil
1 cup chopped onions
3 cloves garlic, minced
2 cups of tomato puree
3 cups water*
1 cup brown rice, quick cooking
1 can kidney beans, washed and drained
1 can chick peas, washed and drained
¼ cup fresh basil
½ tsp. oregano

Heat oil in large saucepan or Dutch oven. Add onions and garlic, cook about 2 minutes. Add remaining ingredients. Bring to a boil. Cover, reduce heat and simmer for 10 minutes.

*May add homemade chicken stock if desired.

Sprinkle individual servings with grated Parmesan cheese.

TOMATO AND CARROT SOUP

1 tablespoon oil
2 medium onions, chopped
½ lb. carrots, sliced
½ cup celery, chopped
½ cup peas
½ lb. tomatoes, peeled
1 bay leaf
1 teaspoon salt
¼ teaspoon pepper
4 cups water

Heat the oil and sauté the onions until transparent. Add the carrots and celery and cook until the onions are golden brown. Add the remaining ingredients and bring to a boil.

Reduce heat, cover and simmer for 45 minutes. Remove bay leaf before serving.

CREAM OF TOMATO SOUP

1 cup milk
2 ½ cups tomatoes
2 tablespoons flour
1 tablespoon sugar
1 thin sliced onion
1 dash pepper
2 tablespoons butter, softened
1 teaspoon salt
1 dash garlic

Heat milk in a saucepan.
Put remaining ingredients in
blender. Cover and puree until smooth. Remove feeder cap and slowly pour the hot milk into the mixture while processing.

POTATO CORN CHOWDER

2 Tbsp. butter
1 onion, diced
½ cup celery, diced
1 cup of potatoes, diced
2 cups water
1 cup of chicken stock (preferably homemade)
1 cup 2% milk or half and half
⅛ tsp. pepper
1 16 oz. can corn, frozen or 6 ears of fresh
2 green onions, sliced for garnish

Melt butter in large sauce pan. Sauté onions, celery and potatoes. Cook until tender.

Add water, chicken stock, milk and pepper and heat thoroughly. Stir in corn. Do not boil. Garnish with green onions. Makes 4 servings

VEGETABLE CHOWDER

½ cup pure olive oil
1 onion, chopped
6 cloves garlic, minced
2 small zucchini, diced
1 small eggplant, diced
1 red pepper, diced
2 ears of fresh corn, cut from cob (or frozen)
1 large potato, diced
4 large ripe tomatoes or 1 large can of crushed tomatoes

Heat oil in large kettle. Add all ingredients, except tomatoes, and sauté. Add fresh or canned tomatoes. Cook until vegetables are tender. If desired, add a cup of small pasta and cook additional 10 minutes. Serve with Parmesan cheese and basil.

PASTA

JEAN N. PETRANTO

LIGHT GNOCCHI

A truly wonderful Gnocchi

6 large potatoes – peeled, cooked and mashed
½ lb. of ricotta
2 Tbsp. melted butter
1 tsp. salt
1 cup flour
3 large egg yolks

In food processor (or by hand), mix flour, eggs, salt, ricotta, mashed potatoes until it forms a soft ball – if dry add 1 more egg yolk – if damp add more flour.

Roll half the dough into a long 1" rope. Cut into 1" slanted pieces. Take fork and press onto dough to create a design. Dough will curl. Do the same with the remaining dough.

Let dry for 2 hours. Cook until tender, about 10-12 minutes. Serves about 8. May freeze.

GARLIC & OIL SAUCE

You can use more or less garlic – whichever you prefer.

½ cup of pure virgin olive oil
4-6 cloves garlic, minced
⅓ cup flat Italian parsley, chopped
½ tsp. dried oregano
1 cup chicken stock
½ tsp. salt

¼ tsp. ground pepper
Romano or Parmesan cheese

Heat oil slightly, cook garlic over low heat until barely golden brown, let it stand. Cooks quickly—Do not overbrown! Stir in parsley, salt, pepper and oregano. Serve over hot linguini fini pasta. Top with cheese as desired.

CHICK PEAS & PASTA

1 lb. of dry chick peas washed & soaked overnight (or 2 cans)
¼ cup pure or virgin oil
3 Tbsp. garlic, minced
1 medium onion, chopped
1 cup celery, chopped
1 potato – cut up in small chunks
½ head cabbage, escarole or savoy cabbage
1 8 oz. can tomato paste
1 medium can pureed tomatoes
Parmesan cheese
Small Pasta

If using dry, cook chick peas until tender – add salt. Set aside.

In large saucepan, heat oil. Sauté garlic, onion and celery until soft. Add tomato paste, 2 cans water, tomato puree, salt and pepper. Stir. Cook about 30 minutes.

Meanwhile, boil cabbage and potatoes until tender. Add cabbage and potatoes to chick peas – cook together for 10 minutes. Drain water from chick pea mixture, saving water. Cook about 20 minutes, adding saved water if needed. Add 1 cup small pasta, cover and shut off flame. Let sit about 10 minutes or until pasta is tender. Serve with parsley and Parmesan cheese.

STUFFED SHELLS OR MANICOTTI

1 lb. of large shells or manicotti
½ lb. ricotta cheese
½ lb. spinach, chopped & cooked, squeeze out water (optional)
3 eggs
½ cup Romano cheese
1 tsp. salt
¼ pepper
⅛ tsp. oregano
¼ tsp. fine fresh garlic, mashed
Spaghetti sauce

Prepare shells or manicotti al dente, drain. Mix all other ingredients together. Fill shells/manicotti with ricotta mixture. Cover the bottom of a large baking dish lightly with sauce. Place shells/manicotti in pan and cover with sauce. Do not layer shells/manicotti, use more pans if needed. Top with grated cheese.

Bake 350° for 45 minutes or until bubbly. Serves 4. May be frozen. Cover with wax paper, then aluminum foil. Let thaw overnight before baking.

BEEF AND SPINACH MANICOTTI

1 small can whole tomatoes
1 lb. ground beef
1 large onion, chopped
4 cloves garlic, minced
½ lb. mushrooms, sliced
½ cup fresh Italian flat parsley
1 tsp. fennel seed (optional)
1 Tbsp. fresh basil (or 1 tsp. dried basil)
2 10 oz. pkg. frozen or 16 oz. fresh spinach
⅓ cup grated Parmesan cheese
2 cups ricotta cheese

14 uncooked manicotti shells
Heat oven 350°. Brown beef, onions and garlic in 10" skillet, stirring often. Drain, put back in skillet.

Stir in tomatoes, mushrooms, basil, parsley and fennel seed. Cook medium low heat about 10 minutes.

Stir ½ of the mixture into a 9 x 13 baking dish. Wash spinach in cold water or drain frozen spinach – squeeze both. Mix spinach, ricotta, Parmesan cheese and season with salt and pepper.

Fill uncooked shells with spinach mixture. Place shells over beef mixture; pour remaining beef mixture on top, covering shells completely.

Sprinkle with Parmesan cheese. Bake, covered, 1½ hours or until shells are tender. Serve with sauce or plain. Serves 7-8.

FETTUCCINE CARBONARA

2 9 oz. packages fresh fettuccine or 1 lb. dry, cooked according to package directions
1 lb. thickly sliced bacon, cut crosswise into strips
½ cup green onions including tops, sliced
¼ cup dry white wine
2 cups heavy cream
¾ cup Romano or Parmesan cheese
3 eggs, lightly beaten
¼ cup parsley, chopped
Freshly grated pepper

While pasta cooks, sauté bacon and onions until lightly brown. Pour off all but ¼ cup of the bacon fat and add wine. Simmer five minutes.

Add 1 ½ cups heavy cream and the cheese. Cook, stirring, until cream starts to bubble and sauce thickens.

Combine remaining ½ cup cream with the eggs, parsley and pepper. Stir into sauce, remove from heat, and toss with fettuccine.

WHITE CLAM SAUCE

1 dozen fresh clams scrubbed clean or 2 large cans whole clams
1 cup Italian flat parsley, chopped
½ cup oil
4 cloves garlic, minced
Cheese, salt, red crushed pepper
Pasta
Parmesan cheese

Shuck clams or open canned clams with juice; set aside. Sauté oil, garlic parsley until silvery. Add juice from 1 can of clams or 1 cup of water, salt and pepper and cook about 10 minutes. Set aside.

Cook pasta. Heat clam juice, add raw clams and cook about 5 minutes. Do not overcook or clams will get rubbery.

Pour over pasta. Sprinkle with cheese, parsley and crushed red pepper if desired.

For a thicker sauce, put 2 Tbsp. flour and ¼ cup clam broth or water in container with lid, shake until blended. Pour into sauce and stir until thickened.

RED CLAM SAUCE

1 dozen fresh scrubbed clean or 2 larges can of whole clams
2 lbs. fresh tomatoes or 1 28 oz. can petite diced or crushed
½ cup parsley
4 cloves garlic, minced
½ tsp. oregano
¼ cup pure virgin oil
½ small can of tomato paste

Put tomatoes in very hot water. Peel off skin, blend in food processor until crushed – set aside.

Sauté oil, garlic, oregano, parsley, paste, crushed tomatoes and 2 cups of water. Simmer about an hour.

Shuck clams or open can – set aside. Steam clams to open. Remove clams from shell and place in sauce. Heat clams for another minute or two. Do not overcook clams or they will get hard.

Serve on Linguini Fini with fresh parsley & cheese. Season to taste.

PORK RIB AND SAUSAGE SAUCE

6 pork ribs
½ lb. hot Italian sausage
¼ cup virgin olive oil
6 cloves garlic, minced
1 small onion, chopped
1 large can tomato paste
3 large cans tomato sauce (fresh tomatoes can be also used)
¼ fresh basil
¼ tsp. baking soda
1 tsp. sugar
Crushed red pepper

Heat large kettle, add cut up ribs and sausage. Brown meat. Add remaining ingredients. Simmer about 3 hours, stirring occasionally.

RED PEPPER SAUCE

My favorite!

2 red peppers, sliced
¼ cup virgin olive oil plus 2 Tbsp.
8 cloves garlic, minced
1 small onion, chopped
2 large cans tomato sauce
1 medium can tomato paste
1 lb. Italian hot sausage
¼ tsp. baking soda
1 tsp. sugar
Parmesan cheese

Sauté peppers in 2 Tbsp. olive oil until soft. Drain oil. Set aside.

In large kettle, heat ¼ cup olive oil. Sauté garlic and onion. Add sauce, paste and 2 cans of water (paste cans).

Heat frying pan with about and inch of water. Cut sausage in 1 **½"** pieces. Cook in water about 10 minutes. Drain water and brown sausage. Add to sauce along with baking soda and sugar. Cook about 1 **½** hours.

Serve with grated Parmesan and Basil Seasoning (recipe follows).

Basil Seasoning:
½ cup fresh basil
4 long hot Italian peppers-roasted, peeled and cut up
¼ cup garlic, minced
Olive oil

Put in small bowl and cover in olive oil. Allow flavors to blend.

MILD MEATBALL SAUCE

Children love this dish!

6-8 meatballs, browned (recipe follows)
1 onion, chopped
6 cloves garlic, minced
¼ cup pure olive oil
1 medium can tomato paste
2 large cans tomato sauce or puree
¼ - ½ cup fresh basil (or 1 tsp. dried)
1 tsp. baking soda
1 ½ tsp. sugar
Crushed red pepper (optional)

In large kettle, heat 2-3 Tbsp. oil. Sauté onions and garlic until silvery. Add tomato paste-2 cans water, 2 cans puree, ½ can water, baking soda, sugar, red pepper and basil. Simmer 2 hours, stirring occasionally. Add meatballs the last 20 minutes.

MEATBALLS

---

1 pound ground beef
1 ½ cups of freshly grated bread crumbs (use recipe in book)
5 cloves garlic, minced
¼ cup fresh parsley
¾ cups grated Parmesan cheese
3 eggs
Salt and pepper to taste

Blend together the garlic, parsley, cheese and eggs. Then combine all ingredients together until thoroughly mixed. Shape into meatballs, the size of your choice.

Fry or broil until brown and add to your sauce during the last fifteen minutes of cooking time. Recipe can be doubled.

MARINARA SAUCE

¼ cup olive oil
1 small onion, minced
6 cloves garlic, minced
2 lbs. fresh ripe tomatoes, peeled and chopped or 2 large cans tomatoes
¼ tsp. sugar
¼ tsp. baking soda
1 cup Italian flat parsley, chopped
Crushed red pepper
Salt

Heat oil in large kettle. Add onion and garlic; sauté until silvery. Add tomatoes, sugar and baking soda to lower acidity. Add parsley, crushed pepper and salt to taste.

Simmer about 1 hour, stirring occasionally.

GREENS OVER PASTA

1 16 oz. package fresh spinach, washed and chopped or dandelion
greens or rappi
½ cup pure olive oil
6 cloves garlic, minced
¼ cup parsley, chopped
3 cups water
Parmesan cheese
Crushed red pepper (optional)
Pasta

In large saucepan sauté spinach, greens or rappi in garlic and olive oil; stirring constantly until tender. Add water and simmer about 15 minutes. Add parsley, salt, pepper and crushed red pepper if desired.

Serve over any type of pasta. Top with grated cheese.

BAKED ZITI IN RED PEPPER SAUCE

1 lb. ziti
½ cup pure olive oil
4 cloves garlic, minced
1 onion, chopped
1 small can of tomato paste
1 large can tomatoes or 8 fresh tomatoes
2 red peppers, chopped
2 Tbsp. fresh basil, chopped
Parmesan cheese

In large sauce pan, heat ¼ cup oil. Sauté garlic and onions together. Add paste, 1 can water, and tomatoes. Cook, stirring occasionally, until slightly thickened, about 1 hour.

Sauté red peppers in remaining ¼ cup oil. Set aside. Cook pasta according to package directions. Drain. Add sauce and put into baking dish. Top with peppers, basil and cheese. Bake 350° for 1 hr.

COMPANY RICE

1 cup of red, green and yellow pepper, chopped
½ cup onions, chopped
3 cloves garlic, minced
1 jalapeno pepper, seeded and minced
1 Tbsp. pure olive oil
1 ½ cups plum tomatoes, diced
¼ tsp. salt
2 cups of cooked white or brown rice
1 can of chick peas, rinsed and drained
1 cup shredded Monterey Jack cheese, divided

In large skillet, heat oil. Sauté peppers, onions, garlic and jalapeno pepper. Cook 5 minutes. Add tomatoes and cook a few more minutes, until tomatoes are soft. Add cooked rice, chick peas, half cup of jack cheese and stir gently.

Place in 1 ½ quart casserole dish and top with remaining cheese. May keep warm in 325° oven until ready to serve.

VEGETABLES

JEAN N. PETRANTO

MUSHROOM-SPINACH SWIRLS

1 (8-ounce) package cream cheese, softened
⅔ cup butter, softened
1 cup plus 1 tablespoon flour
1 cup self rising flour
1 (10-ounce) package frozen chopped spinach
2 Tbsp. butter
2 ½ cups chopped fresh mushrooms
1 cup chopped onion
½ tsp. dried oregano, crushed
½ tsp. salt
½ tsp. lemon juice
⅛ tsp. garlic powder
¼ cup grated nonfat Parmesan cheese
1 egg white
1 Tbsp. water

In a large bowl beat together cream cheese and the ⅔ cup butter. Add 1 cup of the flour and the self rising flour, beat well. Divide dough into two balls; wrap in plastic wrap. Chill 30-60 minutes or until pastry is easy to handle.

For filling, cook spinach according to package directions; drain. Squeeze out excess liquid; set aside.

In a large skillet melt the 2 tablespoons butter. Add mushrooms and onion. Cook and stir over medium heat for 3 minutes or until onion is tender. Add spinach, remaining 1 tablespoon flour, oregano, salt, lemon juice, and garlic powder. Cook and stir until mixture thickens. Stir in Parmesan cheese. Set aside to cool.

On floured surface roll a pastry ball into a 12 x 7-inch rectangle. Spread with half the spinach mixture to within ½ inch of edges. Starting with the short side, roll up the dough and filling, jelly roll style. Moisten edges with water, pinch to seal.

Combine egg white and water. Slice logs into ½ inch thick slices. Place on ungreased baking sheet, brush with egg mixture. Bake 20

31

minutes, cool and serve.

ARTICHOKES FRENCH

1 can of artichokes, drained and washed
½ cup flour
Salt and pepper
2 egg whites, whipped with 2 Tbsp. water
1 lemon-zest and juiced
¼ cup pure olive oil
¼ cup parsley, chopped
¼ cup white wine
3 cloves garlic, minced

Flatten down artichokes with hand. Drench in flour, salt and pepper. Dip in whipped egg white.

Heat oil in skillet. Fry artichokes, turning, until browned. Place in baking dish with remaining ingredients. Bake in 325° degree oven just until heated through.

May double recipe.

ESCAROLE AND BEANS

1 lb. dry cannelloni beans, soak overnight (or use 2 cans)
1 large head of escarole lettuce, washed and chopped
¼ cup virgin olive oil
6 gloves garlic, minced
Salt and pepper to taste
Parmesan cheese
Crushed red pepper

Cook beans until tender. Set aside.

Heat oil in large skillet, sauté garlic briefly. Add escarole and cook until tender. Add beans and water as desired. Season with salt and pepper. Cook until heated through.

Sprinkle with grated cheese and crushed red pepper if desired.

BAKED CABBAGE – CABBAGE LOVERS

1 medium head cabbage, chopped
1 onion, cut into chunks
1 green pepper, cut into chunks
3 stalks celery, cut into chunks
1 small jar pimentos
3 Tbsp. butter
4 Tbsp. flour
1 cup milk
1 cup cheddar cheese, shredded

Sprinkle with buttered bread crumbs

Cover cabbage, onions, peppers, celery and pimentos with water – salt to taste – cook until tender. Drain and place in 9 x 13 pan.

In a separate pan, melt butter and stir in flour. Cook, stirring, a few minutes. Slowly add milk. Cook, stirring constantly, until thickened.

Add shredded cheese. Pour over cabbage, top with bread crumbs.

Bake 350° for 40-45 minutes.

ITALIAN GREEN BEAN STEW

¼ cup oil
1 pkg. fresh or frozen Italian
green beans (flat beans only)
2 large potatoes, cut into chunks
1 onion, diced
6 cloves fresh garlic, minced
½ head romaine lettuce,
chopped (use outer leaves only,
rest may be used for salad)
Crushed red pepper

Cook potatoes until parboiled. Save the water they were cooked in – set aside.

Beans: add 2 Tbsp. oil to skillet and heat. Add half the garlic, sauté briefly. Add beans and lettuce. Sauté until soft. If using fresh beans, boil first until tender.

In a saucepan heat another 2 Tbsp. oil. Sauté onion and remaining garlic, then add beans & potatoes. Add saved potato water, enough to moisten. Season with salt and pepper. Cook until tender, stirring frequently.

ITALIAN TOMATO SALAD

3 medium tomatoes, quartered or 1 container of grape tomatoes
1 slim cucumber, sliced thin
1 small red onion, sliced thin
3 celery stalks, chopped (optional)
3 romaine lettuce leaves, chopped
Handful of Kalamata olives, pitted and cut in half
½ cup fresh basil
Sprinkle of oregano
Salt and pepper

In a large bowl, add all ingredients and mix together. For Christmas, add a handful of sliced radishes and fresh green peas.

Dressing:
¼ cup pure olive oil
¼ cup vinegar or according to taste
Mix well and pour over salad.

ONE PAN VEGGIE RATATOUILLE

½ cup of pure oil
2 cloves garlic, minced
1 large onion, peeled and quartered
4 medium fresh tomatoes – peeled and quartered
1 medium eggplant – cut in chunks
2-4 small zucchini
1 green or red pepper, cut in chunks
Salt & pepper to taste

In large kettle heat oil. Add onion, garlic and tomatoes and sauté until soft. Add remaining vegetables, stirring frequently until tender. Add a little water (for more juice) and season with salt and pepper. Serves 10.

MAIN DISHES

SPECIAL SEAFOOD FRA DIAVOLO

3 Tbsp. pure virgin olive oil
6-10 cloves garlic, minced and divided
1 onion, minced
1 28 oz. can crushed tomatoes
1 tsp. dried oregano, or more if using fresh
3 Tbsp. fresh parsley
½ cup clam juice
¼ tsp. salt
¼ - ½ tsp. cayenne pepper (optional)

8 Cherry Stone Clams, scrubbed clean
8 Mussels, scrubbed (optional)
8 Shrimp, deveined
8 Scallops

1 lb. linguini fini
Fresh basil
Parmesan cheese

In saucepan heat 1 Tbsp. oil and sauté onion and half the garlic briefly. Add tomatoes, tomato paste, 1 can water, spices & clam juice – simmer 1 hour.

In skillet heat 2 Tbsp. oil and sauté remaining garlic briefly. Add clams and mussels (if using) and sauté until shellfish open. Then add shrimp and scallops. Add to sauce and simmer until shrimp and scallops are cooked. If you like it spicy, add cayenne pepper.

Cook linguini fini according to package directions. Place pasta in individual serving bowls and pour sauce and seafood on top.

Serve with fresh basil and Parmesan cheese. Serves 4.

SALMON WITH CHEESE SAUCE

1 lb. fresh or canned salmon
¼ cup soft fresh bread crumbs
2 scallions, chopped
1 Tbsp. butter, melted
1 egg, slightly beaten
¼ cup shredded cheddar or Swiss cheese

If using fresh salmon, brown slightly in small pieces a few minutes – if canned use as is.

In buttered loaf pan add all ingredients.

Bake 375° for 40 minutes. Serve with baked sweet or russet potato.

Cheese Sauce:
1 cup milk
2 Tbsp. butter, melted
2 Tbsp. flour
¼ cup Cheddar or Swiss cheese, grated

Melt butter, add flour, stirring a few minutes. Add milk, stirring constantly until thickened. Add cheese, salt and pepper to taste. Stir until cheese melts.

Pour sauce over salmon. Serves 4-6

BLACKENED CATFISH

6 catfish fillets
2 tsp. paprika
Salt and pepper
1 tsp. onion powder
1 tsp. cayenne pepper (or according to taste)
1 tsp. thyme
1½ tsp. basil
1 stick unsalted butter, plus 3 Tbsp.
4 lemon wedges
Angel hair pasta
2 tsp. lemon pepper marinade (optional)
White wine (optional)

In a small dish combine paprika, salt, pepper, onion powder, cayenne pepper, thyme and basil. Set aside.

Heat 1 stick butter in non-stick pan on high heat. Brown both sides of fillets. Remove from pan and cool. Place on wax paper and sprinkle fillets with spice mix on both sides.

Lower flame - add 3 Tbsp. butter and cook slowly on both sides – 2 minutes per side.

Meanwhile cook angel hair pasta. Pour remaining juices from pan on pasta and serve warm with fillets.

Cook in well ventilated kitchen. If pasta is dry add lemon pepper marinade as well as butter & water.

EGGPLANT PARMESAN

1 or 2 eggplants
3 cups fresh grated bread crumbs
1 cup grated Romano cheese
½ cup flat Italian parsley, chopped
2 eggs, beaten
2 cloves minced garlic
½ cup grated cheese plus a few Tbsp.
½ cup flour
½ cup pure olive oil
1 cup spaghetti sauce

Cut eggplant lengthwise in ½" slices. Salt each slice and let sit while prepping remaining ingredients.

In pie plate or on waxed paper, mix together bread crumbs, Romano cheese, parsley and pepper. Set aside.

Beat egg with garlic, grated cheese and 2-3 Tbsp. water in pie plate. Set aside.

Dip sliced eggplant in flour, egg batter and then prepared breadcrumbs. Brown in hot olive oil, then place in oblong baking dish.

Cover each piece of eggplant with sauce, cheese and parsley. Warm in 325° until heated through, about 10 minutes.

BRACIOLE BEEF ROLL UP

Makes 6-8 individual servings

2 lbs. large sliced beef steak or top round, pounded ¼" thick about 6-8" pieces
2 Tbsp. minced sweet pepper – Red or Green
2 Tbsp. Romano or grated Parmesan cheese
3 Tbsp. flat Italian parsley
2 cloves garlic, minced or crushed
1 tsp. fresh or dry basil
¾ tsp. salt
1 tsp. pepper
¼ cup minced capicola, salami or cooked Italian sausage
3 cup tomato sauce (homemade preferred)
1 egg, beaten
1 small onion, diced
¼ cup olive oil

Lay all pieces of meat flat. Mix remaining ingredients together, except oil. Place on top of flattened meat pieces.

Roll tightly and tie securely with white string. Brown well in oil, drain. Place in spaghetti sauce and slowly cook 2 hours, stirring occasionally, until tender.

Serve with pasta of choice.

BRACIOLA

Makes 1 large
1½ lbs. round steak
Salt and pepper
⅛ tsp. oregano
8 Tbsp. fresh plain bread crumbs
¼ cup Parmesan cheese
1½ Tbsp. grated onion
½ cup parsley, minced
1 clove garlic, minced
1 stalk celery, minced
2 hard boiled eggs – diced
3 strips bacon or pancetta, cooked, crisp, drained
½ cup pepperoni (optional)
Olive oil
Pasta

Lay steak on flat surface. Add salt, pepper, oregano, bread crumbs, cheese, onions, celery, egg, bacon and pepperoni if using.

Roll tightly and tie securely with white string. Heat a little olive oil in a skillet & brown meat roll on all sides. Reduce heat and continue to cook about 1 hour, turning roll occasionally.

Remove from skillet, cut off string, cut into 1" slices. Cover with sauce. Serve with pasta. Garnish with parsley.

CORNED BEEF AND CABBAGE

4 lbs. corned beef – brisket, beef kielbasa or ham
1 large cabbage
6 onions, cut in chunks
6 carrots, cut in chunks
6 potatoes, cut in chunks

Cover meat with cold water. Heat rapidly to boiling than remove scum. Reduce heat. Simmer until tender 3-4 hours.

Prepare vegetables – cut cabbage in 8 pieces.

1 hour before serving skim fat from liquid – add vegetables – cook until tender. Season as desired. Serves 10.

MEAT LOAF SUPREME

1 lb. ground beef
½ lb. ground pork
½ lb. ground veal
2 eggs, slightly beaten
1 cup soft fresh bread crumbs
¼ cup minced onions
1 tsp. tomato sauce
2 Tbsp. light cream
1 tsp. dry mustard
½ cup chili sauce (optional)
Salt and pepper to taste
1 Tbsp. pure olive oil

Mix all ingredients together, except oil. Bake in loaf pan 350° for one hour. Or shape into 4-6 individual loaves. Heat olive oil in heavy skillet. One at a time, brown loaves over medium high heat. Then place all loaves back in skillet and reduce heat to low. Cover and cook 45 minutes, turning loaves..

EASY DEEP ELEGANT BROWN STEW

¼ cup pure olive oil
2 cloves minced garlic
1 tsp. lemon juice
1 small bay leaf
2 lbs. stew beef
3 potato halves
4 carrots, cut into thirds
1 cup celery, cut into 1" pieces
1 cup cooked peas – frozen or fresh
2 Tbsp. flour
¼ cup water – season to taste
1 tsp. salt

Add oil to Dutch oven or large kettle. Add garlic, lemon juice & bay leaf. Add meat and brown on all sides.

Stir in 1½ cups boiling water, reduce heat to low, simmer for 2 hours, stirring occasionally.

Uncover, remove bay leaf. Add potatoes, carrots, celery (if necessary add a little more boiling water) cover, cook on low heat until tender, 30-40 min. Add peas.

Stir flour into cold water to make a paste – Stir into stew to thicken. Add seasoning. Serves 6-8.

VEAL FRENCH

½ to 1 lb. thin veal cutlets
Flour
¼ cup pure olive oil
3 cloves garlic, minced
½ cup Italian parsley, chopped
Juice of 1 large lemon
Salt and pepper to taste
¼ cup white wine (optional)

Pat cutlets in flour. Heat oil in skillet and brown cutlets. Place in baking dish.

To skillet, add garlic, parsley, lemon juice, salt and pepper, a little water or white wine if using. Simmer until reduced slightly.

Pour over cutlets. Sprinkle with a little more parsley if desired. Bake in 325° oven for 20 minutes.

PEPPER TRIPE POT

¼ cup oil
1 onion, chopped
1 green pepper, chopped
1 cup celery, diced
1 lb. fresh tripe, diced, remove fat
1½ quarts boiling water
2 cups beef broth (prefer homemade)
8 peppercorns or black pepper equivalent to taste
1 bay leaf
1 tsp. thyme
¼ cup broken pasta
3 carrots, cut into 1" slices
1½ cup potatoes, diced
1 cup fresh or canned tomatoes

Put tripe in large kettle, cover with water. Boil 5 minutes. Drain.

Heat oil in kettle – add cooked tripe, onions, peppers, celery – cook – stirring over high heat for 5 minutes until browned.

Reduce heat to low, add broth & spices – cook until tender, about 1 hour. Serve piping hot! Serves 4.

DELICIOUS CHUNKY CHILI

3 Tbsp. pure olive oil
3 lb. chunk stewed meat, cut into 1 inch chunks
3 onions, quartered
1 green pepper, diced
2 cloves garlic, minced
1 (8 ounce) can diced tomatoes
1 (6 ounce) can tomato paste
Salt and pepper to taste
3 Tbsp. chili powder
3 cans red kidney beans, drained

Brown meat in oil. Add onions, peppers, garlic, diced tomatoes, and tomato paste. Bring to a boil then add seasonings and cook until tender.

Add kidney beans and cook 5-10 minutes. Serve with cheddar cheese or sour cream if desired.

CHICKEN THIGHS TREAT

An easy dish to make!

4-6 plump thighs, remove skin
¼ cup pure olive oil
2 red peppers, diced
1 green pepper, diced
1 onion, diced
4 cloves garlic, minced
Salt and pepper to taste
2 Tbsp. cornstarch or ½ cup flour

Soak chicken in salt water for 2 hours. Wash well. Heat oil in thick bottomed stainless steel frying pan for 2 minutes. Add dry chicken, brown on both sides, remove from pan.

While pan is still hot, add 2" of water and stir with wooden spoon. Mix and save juice.

Add a little more oil to skillet, sauté peppers, onion and garlic until soft. Place thighs back in skillet, add a little more water & simmer until tender, about 1 hour. Thighs may also be baked in 325° oven.

Heat juice. Mix cornstarch or flour with a little water to make a paste. Add paste to juice, stirring until thickened.

Serve gravy over mashed potatoes & chicken. May place chicken in casserole dish, top with gravy, and keep warm until ready.

EASY BREAKFAST MENU

½ lb. beef kielbasa

Hash Browns:
2 grated potatoes
¼ cup olive oil

1 bunch green onions

Omelet:
4 eggs
1 dash milk
salt and pepper to taste

Brown kielbasa over low heat and set aside. Sauté potatoes and green onions in olive oil until brown and set aside.

Beat eggs with a little milk and add salt and pepper. Cook omelet in non-stick pan.

Serve all ingredients together.

LUNCH MENU

Tuna Melt: (2 sandwiches)
Sliced cheddar cheese
1 can tuna
2 Stalks celery (chopped)
2 sprigs parsley (chopped)
3 tablespoons mayonnaise
2 hard boiled eggs (chopped)
1 small onion (chopped)
Salt and pepper to taste

Salad:
1 Cucumber (sliced)
1 large tomato (chopped)
Small red onion (chopped)
⅛ cup oil
⅛ cup wine vinegar
1 glove garlic (minced)
1 dash oregano
Salt and pepper to taste

Mix tuna, celery, parsley, eggs, mayonnaise, onion and salt and pepper.

Place cheese on bread and spread mixture. Butter both sides and heat on non-stick pan until golden brown.

Add all ingredients for salad in a large bowl and mix well. Serve salad with sandwich.

DESSERTS

JEAN N. PETRANTO

JEAN'S ITALIAN COOKIES

1 cup sugar
1 cup of shortening or margarine
3 whole eggs
1 cup milk
2 Tbsp. lemon juice
3½ cups of unbleached flour
½ cup sour cream (optional)
¼ cup baking powder

I double the recipe to freeze some.

In a large bowl add sugar and eggs. Beat together. Add baking powder to flour – mix. Add little at a time with milk, oil (slowly), lemon juice, sour cream – mix until blended

Roll out on floured board into any shape. I like knots or round 2" cookies.

Bake 350° for 8-10 minutes. Cool and frost.

Lemon Butter Frosting:
1 cup confectioner's sugar
1 drop of milk for spreading
3 Tbsp. melted butter
1 tsp. lemon or orange juice or extract
Pinhead candies
Lemon or orange zest

Beat first four ingredients together. Spread on baked cookies or sprinkle with extra sugar. Sprinkle with small pinhead candies or lemon or orange zest.

ORANGE DROP COOKIES

1 cup sugar
1 cup shortening
1 cup sour milk or sour cream
1 Tbsp. baking soda
2 eggs
4 cups unbleached flour
1 tsp. baking powder
pinch of salt
Juice and rind from one orange

Cream together shortening, sugar and eggs – add remaining ingredients – mix thoroughly. Drop by teaspoon onto greased baking sheet.

Bake 375° for 10-15 minutes

Orange Frosting:
½ cup butter, softened
3 cups confectionary sugar
1 tsp. vanilla
orange juice

Blend together butter, sugar and vanilla. Add orange juice until it reaches a spreading consistency. Sprinkle with orange rind.

CUCIDATI (ITALIAN FIG COOKIES)

Dough
5 cups of flour
3 Tbsp. baking powder
1½ tsp. salt
1 cup sour cream
2 eggs
1½ cups sugar
½ cup oil
2 tsp. vanilla
½ cup milk
1 egg white

In a large bowl add flour, baking powder and salt and mix. Add sour cream, sugar, eggs, oil and vanilla. Mix well until it forms a ball. Knead 2 minutes, if sticky add more flour, if dry add a little milk. Set aside.

Fig Filling
3 lbs. dried dark figs, washed, remove stems
2 lbs. dried light figs, washed, remove stems
1 lb. light raisins
1 lb. dark raisins
1 lb. pitted dates, chopped
1 lb. almonds
1 lb. hazelnuts
1½ lbs. walnuts
1 large orange, chopped in food processor with peel
¼ - ½ cup brandy
1 lb. pure honey

Put nuts in oven at 350° on cookie sheet. Roast 10 minutes or until lightly toasted. Remove from oven. Chop into small pieces in food processor or grinder.

Put chopped nuts in large kettle with thick bottom. Add figs, raisins, dates, brandy, honey and orange (all chopped). Cook over medium heat (be very careful it does not stick), stirring constantly for 15 minutes or until bubbly. Remove from heat and cool.

On a floured board divide dough into baseball size pieces and set aside. Roll one ball at a time until it's a large round sheet. Have filling ready a little at a time in a small bowl. Add filling in 3 rows all the way across leaving about ½" on each side of row.

Brush with beaten egg white around edge of dough and roll into a long string about 1-1½" thick. With sharp knife cut into 1½-2" diagonal pieces. Flatten slightly.

Place on greased cookie sheet, 1 – 2 inches apart. Bake 350° 8- 10 minutes until light in color – Do Not Over Brown.

Brush some cookies with egg white and sprinkle with decorations. Some may be frosted with the following recipe and some may be kept plain.

You can also make rope into horseshoe shapes or round or long bars. Leftover filling may be frozen.

Frosting:
3 cups confectionary sugar
4 Tbsp. melted butter
1 tsp. vanilla or orange juice

Beat until well mixed.

PFEFFERNUSSE COOKIES

3 cups sugar
1 cup butter
3 eggs
1 cup honey
½ cup brandy

Sift Together
8 cups flour
1 Tbsp. baking soda
1 Tbsp. cloves
1 Tbsp. cardamom
1 Tbsp. cinnamon

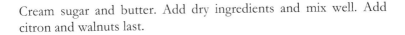

½ cup chopped citron
1½ cup chopped walnuts

Cream sugar and butter. Add dry ingredients and mix well. Add citron and walnuts last.

Roll good size tablespoons of dough into balls. Place on ungreased cookie sheet. Bake 350° for 15 minutes. Roll in powdered sugar while warm.

DELICIOUS DATE COOKIES

1 cup dates, chopped
½ cup water
1 egg
½ cup brown sugar
½ cup butter
¼ cup milk
1 ½ cups flour
½ tsp. salt
½ tsp. baking powder
¼ tsp. baking soda

½ cup nuts, chopped

Cook dates in boiling water for 5 minutes. Set aside 2 teaspoons dates for frosting.

Stir in eggs, sugar, butter, and dry ingredients. Add nuts to mixture. Drop 1 teaspoon size mixture onto cookie sheet. Bake 375° for 8-10 minutes.

Frosting:
Beat together 3 tablespoons butter, 1 ½ cups powdered sugar, ½ teaspoon milk and reserved dates.
Spread evenly over cookies.

MEATBALL COOKIES

1 cup shortening
1 cup milk
8 oz. cream cheese
1 tsp. vanilla
1¼ cup sugar
1 cup chocolate chips
4½ cups flour
5 tsp. baking powder
½ cup cocoa
½ tsp. cinnamon
¼ tsp. nutmeg
¼ tsp. cloves

Mix all ingredients in a large bowl to create a soft dough. Refrigerate 1 hour. Roll dough into balls the size of walnuts.

Bake on greased cookie sheet at 375° for 15 minutes.

HOLIDAY FRUIT COOKIES

1 cup shortening
2 cups packed brown sugar
2 eggs
½ cup rolled oats
3 ½ cups sifted flour
2 tsp. baking powder
1 tsp. cinnamon
½ tsp. nutmeg
½ lb. chopped figs
½ tsp. salt
½ cup milk
1 cup chopped walnuts and almonds
1 cup chopped dates

Cream shortening and brown sugar together. Beat in eggs. Add rolled oats. Sift flour, baking powder, cinnamon, nutmeg, and salt together. Add to creamed mixture alternately with milk. Stir in 1 cup chopped nuts, dates, and figs.

Drop rolled teaspoons of batter onto a baking sheet. Bake at 375° for about 10-12 minutes or until golden brown. Remove and cool.

CHOCOLATE NUTTY COOKIES

¾ cup packed brown sugar
½ cup sugar
1 cup softened butter
1 egg
1½ tsp. vanilla
2¼ cup unbleached flour
1 tsp. baking soda
½ tsp. salt
1 cup coarsely chopped nuts
8 oz. chocolate bars broken into ¼" pieces

In a large bowl combine sugar, brown sugar, butter, eggs & vanilla. Beat at medium speed or mix thoroughly by hand – 2 minutes.

Add flour, baking soda, salt – keep beating until well mixed – 2 minutes by hand. Add walnuts and chocolate pieces.

Drop by tablespoon 2" round onto cookie sheet – 2" apart. Bake 375° for 9-11 minutes. Cool before removing from sheet.

Serve plain, frosted or with powdered sugar.

CHEWY CHOCOLATE CHIP COOKIES

3 eggs
1 tsp. vanilla
2 stick butter, softened
2½ cups flour
2 tsp. baking soda
1 tsp. salt
1 tsp. cinnamon
1 cup brown sugar
1 cup granulated sugar
1 cup raisins
1 cup walnuts
1 cup semi-sweet chocolate chips

Mix all ingredients together. Drop from teaspoon onto greased baking sheet.

Bake 350° for 8-10 minutes.

COCONUT MACAROONS

2 egg whites
⅓ cup sugar
2 tsp. flour
1 dash salt
¼ tsp. almond extract
2 cups coconut

Heat oven to 325°. Grease and lightly flour cookie sheet. In medium bowl, beat egg whites slowly. Add sugar, flour, salt and almond extract; blend well. Stir in coconut.

Drop dough by tablespoons 2 inches apart onto prepared cookie sheet. Bake for 13-17 minutes or until set and lightly browned. Immediately remove from cookie sheet; cool completely.

COCONUT SOUR CREAM COOKIES

½ cup shortening
1 tsp. vanilla
1 ½ cups brown sugar
2 eggs, beaten
½ tsp. salt
2 ½ cups flour, sifted
2 tsp. baking powder
1 tsp. baking soda
1 cup sour cream
1 cup coconut
½ to 1 cup coconut, toasted

Combine shortening, vanilla, brown sugar, eggs, flour, baking soda, salt, coconut, sour cream, mixing well.

Drop dough by teaspoon size onto cookie sheet. Bake at 375° for 8-10 minutes or until lightly browned. Brush cookie with egg and sprinkle on toasted coconut.

SURE PROOF PIE CRUST

Try a food processor – what could be easier!

3 cups unbleached flour
⅔ cup soft butter
⅔ cup Crisco
1½ tsp. salt
5-8 Tbsp. cold water

Put flour, salt, butter, Crisco in food processor – blend until crumbly. Add cold water a little at a time until it forms a ball, mixing about 2 minutes.

Chill 10 minutes and roll into pie plates. Makes 2 pie crusts.

Helpful Hints for Pie Crust—

Make 3 or 4 in glass pie plates. I like to use glass so you can see if the crust is brown & baked well enough. Stack them up with wax paper between. Freeze some for later use.

Always put foil around all fruit pie crusts to prevent over browning and to get an even color.

To bake a shell, prick with fork & bake at 400° with a glass cover in the center so crust won't shift. Cook 10 minutes, removing cover after 5 minutes. Cook until golden brown.

APRICOT CHEESE PIE

Crust:
1 ½ cups of vanilla wafers, crushed
⅓ cup butter, melted
1 tsp. cinnamon

Filling:
1 can of apricots or fresh
1 pkg. lemon gelatin
1 ½ Tbsp. lemon juice
1 tsp. lemon zest
½ lb. of cream cheese
Whipped cream
Nuts, crushed nutmeg

Mix together crushed wafers, melted butter and cinnamon. Press firmly into the bottom and sides of a 9" spring form pan. Bake at 400° until lightly browned.

Drain the apricots and reserve the liquid. Add enough water to the liquid to make up to 1 ½ cups. Add lemon gelatin and heat until gelatin is dissolved. Add the lemon juice and zest and chill until it starts thickening.

Soften the cream cheese and mix with the cheese mixture. Pour into the prepared pie crust and chill until firm.

Top with whipped cream, crushed nuts and a little nutmeg!

PEAR PIE

2 pie crusts
6-8 sliced thin pears
2 Tbsp. corn starch
1 Tbsp. ground cinnamon
1 cup sugar
⅛ tsp. nutmeg
1 tsp. lemon juice
1 tsp. butter, softened
1 large egg white, slightly beaten

Grease 9" or 10" pie plate. Put crust in the pie plate, overlapping about 2". Set crust in place.

Slice pears into bowl. Add remaining ingredients, except egg white, and mix together.

Pour into pie dish, top with lattice crust and flute crust evenly. Brush egg white around crust. Wrap foil around edges of crust.

Bake 400° for 20-30 minutes.

RASPBERRY OR CHERRY PIE

Pastry for two 9" pie crusts
1 10 oz. package frozen berries, thawed and drained
¾ cup sugar
3 Tbsp. corn starch
1 Tbsp. butter
½ tsp. cinnamon

Lay in bottom crust. Mix all ingredients together gently and pour into crust. Put on top crust, and flute. Place foil around edges of crust.
Bake 400° for 40-45 minutes until lightly browned and bubbly.

ORANGE VELVET PIE

¼ cup cold water
2 packets unflavored gelatin
½ cup boiling water
3 eggs
¾ cup sugar
1 dash of salt
½ inch sliced lemon, peeled
1 6-ounce can orange concentrate
2 Tbsp.. sugar for egg whites
¾ cup ship cream
1 9" chocolate wafer crumb crust
Chocolate bits for garnish

Prepare crust. Soften gelatin in cold water in blender. Add hot water, cover and process at stir until gelatin is dissolved. Add egg yolks, sugar, salt, lemon, and orange concentrate. Mix until smooth.

Beat egg whites until foamy, gradually add 2 tablespoons sugar, continue to beat until stiff.

Fold the orange mixture into the egg whites. Pour into prepared crust. Chill until set. Garnish with chocolate chip bites.

CHOCOLATE CHEESE PIE

1 cup evaporated milk
1 cup semi- sweet chocolate chips
2 egg yolks
⅓ cup sugar
1 8 ounce package cream cheese
1 9" graham cracker crumb crust

Pour ½ cup milk into an ice cube try, place in freezer until ice crystals form around edges. Heat remaining ½ cup milk. Pour chocolate chips and hot milk into blender and shred until smooth. Add egg yolks, sugar, then cream cheese pieces. Lastly add chilled milk and blend until creamy.

Pour into pie crust, cover and refrigerate until firm. Garnish with whip cream and a few chocolate chips.

CUSTARD PIE

1 9" pie crust
4 slightly beaten eggs
½ cup sugar
½ tsp. salt
½ tsp. vanilla
⅛ tsp. almond extract
2 ½ cups scalded milk
Nutmeg

Chill pie shell while making filling. Blend eggs, sugar, salt vanilla and almond extract. Gradually stir in scalded milk. Pour into pie shell. Sprinkle with nutmeg.

Bake at 400° for 25-30 minutes or until knife comes out clean.

PEACH PIE

2 lbs. fresh peaches or 2-16 oz. canned peaches
2 Tbsp. flour
¼ tsp. nutmeg
2 Tbsp. butter
2 Tbsp. lemon juice
½ tsp. grated orange peel
⅛ tsp. almond extract
Pastry for two 9" pie crusts

Drain or peel peaches – slice.

In bowl mix flour, spices, lemon, butter and almond extract. Add peaches to mixture.

Lay bottom crust in pie plate. Pour in peach mixture. Set in evenly and moisten edges of bottom crust with water. Sprinkle a bit more flour on top of peach mixture. Put on top crust. Press edges together and flute.

Place foil around edges. Put 4 slits in center of crust to vent. Bake 400° for 40-45 minutes.

PEANUT BUTTER PIE

1 9" unbaked pie crust
3 cups milk
4 Tbsp. flour
3 Tbsp. corn starch
3 egg yolks
½ cup sugar
½ tsp. salt
2 tsp. butter
1 tsp. vanilla
½ cup peanut butter

In blender, mix all ingredients until smooth. Pour into pie crust. Place on bottom shelf of oven. Bake at 400° for 30-40 minutes.

May serve with a scoop of chocolate ice cream or ribbon with chocolate sauce.

CREAMY BANANA PIE

1 package unflavored gelatin
¼ cup cold water
¾ cup sugar
¼ cup cornstarch
½ tsp. salt
2 ¾ cups milk
4 egg yolks, beaten
2 Tbsp. butter
1 Tbsp. vanilla extract
4 medium firm bananas
1 cup heavy cream, whipped
1 pasty shell (10-inches) baked
Juice and grated peel of 1 lemon
½ cup apple jelly

Soften gelatin in cold water, set aside. In a saucepan, combine sugar, cornstarch and salt. Blend in the milk, egg yolks; cook over low heat, stirring constantly, until thickened and bubbly, about 20-25 minutes. Remove from heat, stir in softened gelatin until dissolved. Stir in butter and vanilla. Cove the surface of custard with plastic wrap and chill until no longer warm.

Slice 3 bananas, fold into custard with whipped cream. Spoon into pie shell. Chill until set, about 4-5 hours.

Shortly before serving time, place lemon juice in a small bowl and slice the remaining banana into it. Melt jelly in a saucepan over low heat. Drain banana, pat dry, and arrange on top of pie. Brush banana with jelly. Sprinkle with lemon peel.

HUMMINGBIRD CAKE

2 cups sugar
3 eggs – slightly beaten
3 cups unbleached flour
1 tsp. salt
1 tsp. baking soda
1 tsp. ground cinnamon
¾ cup vegetable oil
1 cup chopped pecans
2 bananas (ripe, mashed)
1 can crushed pineapple with juice
½ tsp. vanilla

Whisk together sugar and eggs. Mix dry ingredients together: flour, salt, soda and cinnamon. Add vanilla, oil, pineapple, bananas and mix well.

Grease and flour two 9" pans; divide batter in pans. Bake at 350° for 25-30 minutes or until lightly browned. Cool on rack. Frost.

Frosting:
1 8 oz. package cream cheese
½ cup butter
1 tsp. vanilla

Frost outside of cake and between layers or use pineapple filling.

Pineapple Filling:
1 medium can crushed pineapple
2 heaping Tbsp. cornstarch
2 Tbsp. sugar

Drain juice from pineapple into a small sauce pan. Add cornstarch and sugar. Heat, stirring, until thickened. Remove from heat and add pineapple. Let cool.

BOSTON CREAM CAKE

4 eggs, separated
Custard Filling:
1 cup sugar
3 egg yolks
4 Tbsp. hot water
2 Tbsp. flour
1 cup flour
1 Tbsp. cornstarch
1 tsp. baking powder
½ cup confection sugar
⅛ tsp. salt
2 cups milk
1 tsp. vanilla
2 Tbsp. butter

Beat egg yolks and sugar until think and light yellow colored. Add water and sifted dry ingredients. Stir in vanilla.

Beat egg whites until stiff. Fold into mixture.

Butter and flour two 8-inch cake pans. Pour in cake mixture and bake at 350° for 20 minutes. Cool.

In the top of a double boiler, mix together the egg yolks, flour, cornstarch, sugar, milk and butter. Place over simmering water and cook, stirring occasionally, until mixture is thick and smooth. Cool.

Spread custard between the two layers and sprinkle confectioners sugar on top.

PERFECT CHOCOLATE CAKE

2 cups sugar
2 eggs
2 tsp. vanilla
½ cup vegetable oil
1 cup boiling water
1¾ cup flour
¾ cup cocoa
1½ tsp. baking powder
1½ tsp. baking soda
1 tsp. salt
1 cup milk

Mix together – pour into 9 x 13 greased pan. Bake 350° for 30-35 minutes.

For extra moist cake, add 1 cup cherry pie filling.

CHOCOLATE SAUCE

Good on cream puffs!

½ lb. dark chocolate
1 cup sugar
3 tablespoons butter
1 large can evaporated milk
1 egg, beaten

Melt the chocolate in the top of a double boiler over simmering water.

Mix in the sugar, butter and evaporated milk. Cook for three minutes. Beat the egg and add. Remove from heat and cool.

To freeze: Pour into a plastic container leaving ½ inch (1 cm) of space at the top to allow for expansion of liquid during freezing.

Cover, seal, label and freeze.

To serve: Allow to thaw a little to make it easier to remove from the container. Put into the top of a double boiler and heat gently, stirring constantly.

SWEET CHOCOLATE GLAZE

¾ cup sugar
2 tablespoons cornstarch
1 cup water
1 dash salt
2 squares German sweet cooking chocolate, cut up
1 ½ tsp. vanilla

In small saucepan combine the sugar and sweet cooking chocolate. Cook and stir until chocolate is melted and mixture is thickened. Cook and stir 2 minutes more. Remove from heat; stir in vanilla.

Cover surface with clear plastic wrap or waxed paper. Let stand 10-15 minutes or till slightly cooled and of spreading consistency.

APPLE CAKE

4 cups fresh apples, diced
½ cup vegetable oil
2 tsp. vanilla
1 tsp. salt
1 cup chopped nuts
2 cups flour
1 tsp. cinnamon
2 cups sugar
2 eggs, beaten
2 tsp. baking soda

1. Mix apples and sugar thoroughly.
2. Add vegetable oil, nuts, eggs and vanilla.
3. Mix and add flour, baking soda, salt and cinnamon.
4. Bake in greased 9 x 13 pan for 1 hour or until it shrinks from edges of pan. Serve plain, iced, or with whipped cream.

APPLE SPICE CAKE

Good for picnics

4 cups apples, peeled, cored, and chopped
1 tsp. nutmeg
½ cup firmly packed brown sugar
¾ tsp. all spice
¼ cup butter, melted
½ tsp. cloves
3 tsp. cinnamon
½ cup cooking oil
2 cups flour
6 eggs, separated
1 ¼ cups sugar
½ cup water
1 Tbsp. baking powder
1 tsp. vanilla

1 tsp. salt
1 cup chopped walnuts
½ tsp. baking soda
¼ tsp. cream of tartar

In medium bowl, stir together 2 cups of apples, brown sugar, butter and 2 teaspoons of cinnamon. Spread evenly over bottom of 10- inch tube pan.

In small bowl mix together 1¾ cups of flour, sugar, baking powder, salt, soda, nutmeg, allspice, and cloves. Add oil, egg yolks, water and vanilla. Beat until satiny smooth.

In small bowl stir the remaining ¼ cup flour, 2 cups apples, 1 teaspoon cinnamon and nuts together until apples are coated. Fold apple mixture into egg yolk mixture.

In large bowl beat eggs whites with cream of tarter until stiff but not dry. Gently fold yolk mixture into egg whites just until blended. Turn into prepared pan.

Bake in 350° degree oven for 1 hour and 10-15 minutes or until top springs back when lightly touched. Invert pan and cool for 5 minutes. Loosen edges with spatula and turn out cake onto cake plate or serving platter to complete cooling.

CHOCOLATE SWIRL CHEESECAKE WITH RASPBERRY TOPPING

4 chocolate wafers, crushed
Thick yogurt (recipe follows)
1 package (8ounces) light cream cheese, softened
⅔ cup sugar
¼ cup skim milk
2 Tbsp. flour
2 tsp. vanilla
3 egg whites
1 Tbsp. cocoa
1 tsp. chocolate extract
Raspberry topping (Recipe follows)

Heat oven to 300°. Spray pan with cooking spray. Sprinkle chocolate wafer crumbs on bottom of pan. Beat thick yogurt and light cream cheese in medium bowl until smooth. Add sugar, milk, flour, vanilla, and egg whites. Beat until smooth.

Place 1 cup batter in small bowl. Beat in cocoa and chocolate extract until blended. Carefully spread vanilla batter over crumbs in pan. Drop chocolate batter by the spoonful onto vanilla batter. Swirl through batter with metal spatula for marbled effect, being careful not to touch bottom.

Bake 1 hour. Turn off oven; leave cheesecake in oven for 30 minutes. Remove from oven, cool 15 minutes. Prepare raspberry topping, spread over cheesecake. Cove and refrigerate at least 3 hours.

Thick Yogurt:
4 cups plain nonfat yogurt

Line 6-inch strainer with basket-style paper coffee filter or double-thickness cheesecloth. Place strainer over bowl. Spoon 4 cups plain nonfat yogurt into strainer.

Cover strainer and bowl and refrigerate for at least 12 hours. Drain liquid from bowl, if necessary, before going to bed. If you have placed the strainer into a deep bowl, you may not have to drain off any liquid. In the morning, discard liquid. Thick yogurt is now ready to use.

Raspberry Topping:
1 package (10 ounces) frozen raspberries in light syrup, thawed, drained, and juice reserved
¼ cup sugar
2 tablespoons cornstarch

Add enough water to reserved juice to measure 1 ¼ cups. Mix sugar and cornstarch in 1½ quarts saucepan. Stir in juice mixture and raspberries.

Heat to boil over medium heat, stirring frequently. Boil and stir 1 minute; cool.

APPLE CRISP

4 cups apples, sliced
½ cup oatmeal
⅓ cup margarine or butter, softened
⅔ cup brown sugar
¾ tsp. cinnamon
½ cup flour
¾ tsp. nutmeg

Place sliced apples in greased 8 x 8 square pan. Blend remaining ingredients until mix is crumbly. Spread over apples. Bake in 375° oven for 30-35 minutes or until apples are tender and crust is golden brown. Serve with ice cream or cream.

ULTIMATE CARROT CAKE

4 eggs
2 cups sugar
1½ cups vegetable oil
2 tsp. vanilla
3 cups sifted flour
2 tsp. baking soda
1 tsp. baking powder
2 tsp. cinnamon
¼ tsp. cloves
¼ tsp. nutmeg
3 cups ground carrots
1 cup raisins
1 cup crushed pineapple
1 cup walnuts

Mix together. Pour into a 9 x 13 baking dish. Bake 350° for 40-55 minutes. Frost with cream cheese frosting. See Hummingbird Cake for recipe. Garnish with shredded carrots.

FRUIT COBBLER

¼ cup butter, softened
½ cup sugar
1 egg
½ cup milk
1 cup flour
2 tsp. baking powder
dash of salt
1 tsp. vanilla
2 cups sliced fresh peaches or any other fruit
⅓ cup honey
1 cup boiling water
1 Tbsp. butter or margarine

Cream butter and sugar together. Add egg, beat well. Stir in milk. Sift together: flour, baking powder and salt. Add to butter mixture. Stir in vanilla. Spoon evenly into greased 9 x 13 baking dish.

Mix together fruit, honey, boiling water and 1 Tbsp. butter. Pour on top. Bake 375° for 40-45 minutes.

BANANA SQUARES

2 eggs, separated
⅔ cup shortening
1 ½ cups sugar
1 cup mashed bananas
1 ½ cups flour
1 tsp. baking soda
¼ cup sour milk
½ tsp. vanilla extract
½ cup chopped walnuts, optional

In a small mixing bowl, beat egg whites until soft peaks form; set aside.

In a large mixing bowl, cream shortening and sugar. Beat in egg yolks; mix well. Add bananas.

Combine flour and baking soda; add to cream mixture alternately with milk, beating well. Add vanilla and fold in egg whites.

Fold in nuts if desired. Pour into a greased pan. Bake at 350° for 45-50 minutes. Cool on a wire rack.

Garnish with a dollop of whipped cream and some banana slices.

RASPBERRY CHEESE SQUARES

Crust:
1 ½ cups graham crackers, crushed
1 teaspoon cinnamon
½ cup butter, melted

Filling:
Raspberry jam
½ cup brown sugar
1 ½ tsp. cornstarch
½ tsp. cinnamon
¾ lb. cream cheese
¼ tsp. salt
1 Tbsp. lemon rind, grated
2 Tbsp. lemon juice
3 eggs, separated
1 cup sour cream
¼ cup sugar

For crust, mix together graham crackers, cinnamon, and melted butter. Firmly press on the bottom of a buttered 7 x 10" pie tin. Spread a thick layer of raspberry jam on the crumb crust.

Mix the brown sugar with the cornstarch and cinnamon. Soften the cream cheese and mix with the brown sugar mixture. Add the salt, lemon rind and lemon juice and mix well.

Lightly beat the egg yolks and stir into the cream cheese mixture with the sour cream. Beat the egg whites until frothy, then add the sugar slowly and continue beating until stiff. Fold into the cream cheese mixture. Pour over the prepared crust and smooth out.

Bake at 350° for ½ hour. Reduce the heat to 300° and bake for another 35 minutes. Turn off the heat and leave in the oven until cooled. Cut into squares and serve.

PINEAPPLE CHEESECAKE

Pastry:
1 cup flour
¼ cup
1/3 cup butter
1 egg yolk
½ tablespoon vanilla

Filling:
2 (8 ounce) packages
cream cheese
4 tablespoons flour
4 eggs
1 ¼ cups sugar

Glaze:
4 tablespoons sugar
1 tablespoon butter
1 ¼ Tbsp. cornstarch
1 can crushed pineapple
¼ cup milk

Mix together all pastry ingredients then spread in pan. Mix all filling ingredients and pour on top of pastry.

Bake 450° for 10 minutes. Then reduce heat to 350° and bake 1½ hours. Turn off heat and leave in oven for ½ hour.

Mix together sugar, cornstarch, milk and butter. Sauté in pan until thick. Stir in pineapple. Stir constantly over medium lot heat until smooth and thick. Spread glaze over cooled cake.

CREAM PUFF PASTRY

1 cup milk
pinch of salt
2 Tbsp. sugar
1 cup flour
4 eggs
½ cup butter, melted

Combine milk, salt and sugar in sauce pan and heat until it comes to a boil. Remove from heat and stir in flour and butter. Let cool 5 minutes.

Put in food processor or beat with mixer at high speed. Add eggs one at a time, process between each egg.

Drop 1 Tbsp. of mixture onto cookie sheet. Bake 350° for 8-10 minutes or until light brown. Cool.

Fill cream puffs just before serving or no more than 3 hours ahead. May drizzle with chocolate sauce or chocolate glaze.

Custard Filling:
2 cups milk
3 Tbsp. cornstarch
3 Tbsp. sugar
3 egg yolks, beaten
1 Tbsp. butter
1 tsp. vanilla

Place milk, cornstarch and sugar in sauce pan. Cook over medium heat, stirring constantly. As it begins to thicken, beat in egg yolks. Add butter and vanilla. Cook until it bubbles 2-3 times. Cool.

Ricotta Filling:
1 lb. ricotta
3 Tbsp. sugar
1 ½ cups powdered sugar
Mix in blender.

LAYERED BANANA PUDDING

⅓ cup flour
⅔ cup packed brown sugar
2 cups milk
2 egg yolks, beaten
2 Tbsp. butter or margarine
1 tsp. vanilla extract
1 cup heavy cream, whipped
4 to 6 firm bananas, sliced
Chopped walnuts optional

In a medium saucepan, combine the flour and brown sugar; stir in milk. Cook and stir over medium heat until thickened and bubbly; cook and stir 1 minute more.

Remove from heat. Gradually stir about 1 cup hot mixture into egg yolks. Return all to the saucepan. Bring to a gentle boil; cook and stir 2 minutes.

Remove from heat, stir in butter and vanilla. Cool to room temperature, stirring occasionally.

Fold in the whipped cream. Layer ⅓ of the pudding into a glass bowl. Top with all the bananas. Repeat layering.

Top with remaining pudding. Sprinkle with nuts if desired. Cover and chill at least 1 hour.

ORANGE CRANBERRY MUFFINS

1 egg
1 cup milk
¼ cup vegetable oil
2 cups flour
¼ cup sugar
2 level Tbsp. baking powder
½ tsp. salt
1 cup fresh cranberries, halved
1 Tbsp. orange peel, grated

Beat egg, milk, cranberries, and oil together. Add all other ingredients and stir.

Fill greased muffin tins ⅔ way full. Bake at 400° for 20 minutes or until brown. Remove and cool on wire rack.

FREEZER BUNS

5 ¼- 6 ¼ cups flour, sifted
1/3 cup sugar
1 tsp. salt
½ tsp. lemon peel, grated
2 packages (¼ ounce each) active dry yeast
1 cup butter, softened
1 ⅓ cups warm water
2 eggs, room temperature

Cheese and/or date-nut filling
Confection sugar

In large bowl, combine 1 ½ cups flour, sugar, salt, lemon peel and dissolved active dry yeast. Add butter. Gently add water to dry ingredients and beat 2 minutes at medium speed.

Add eggs and ⅓ cup flour. Beat at high for 2 minutes. Stir in enough additional flour to make a soft dough. Cover and let rest for 20 minutes.

Divide dough into 3 equal pieces. Roll each piece into an 8-inch square. Cut each square into 8 1-inch strips. Twist each strip and coil in center, sealing ends underneath. Make wide indentation at center of each coil. Spoon desired fillings (recipes follow) into each indentation. Place on greased baking sheet.

Cover loosely with plastic wrap, freeze until firm. Transfer to plastic and freeze up to 4 weeks.

Place on ungreased sheet and thaw. Let rise in warm place. Bake at 375° for 15-20 minutes or until evenly browned. Let cool before serving.

Date-Nut Filling:
2 cups pitted dates
½ cup water
½ cup walnuts, chopped

In a saucepan combine dates and water. Bring to boil over high heat. Reduce heat, cover, and simmer until water is absorbed. Stir in nuts.

Cheese Filling:
2 packages (8 ounces each) cream cheese, softened
½ cup sugar
1 tablespoon grated lemon peel
2 egg whites

Combine cheese, sugar and lemon peel in a bowl. Mix until well blended and smooth. Gradually add in egg whites, stirring until smooth.

QUICK CINNAMON ROLLS

3 tablespoons sugar
½ teaspoon cinnamon
1 package fast-acting dry yeast
½ cup warm milk
½ cup butter, melted
2 eggs
½ teaspoon salt
½ cup sour cream
3 cups flour

Topping:
½ cup dark corn syrup
¼ cup brown sugar
¼ cup butter, melted
⅔ cups chopped nuts
2-3 Tbsp. melted butter

Combine 1 tablespoon sugar with cinnamon. Add yeast and milk. Set aside.

Beat butter with remaining sugar. Add eggs, salt, and sour cream and beat well. Add yeast mixture and beat to blend.

Place flour in a bowl, make a well in the center and add the liquid mixture. Mix with a wooden spoon, making wider and wider circles. Beat well. Let the dough rest 5 minutes. Dough should be firm enough to roll into balls but still a little sticky.

Preheat oven to 350°. Combine topping ingredients and spread topping in the bottom of a 9-inch round baking pan. Divide the dough into 12 equal portions and roll them into balls. Place them in the pan and gently press the tops to flatten them a little. Cover the pan with plastic and let the rolls rise 20 minutes. Brush the rolls with melted butter and bake for 20-25 minutes or until they are browned and puffed.

FRESH APPLESAUCE

¼ cup liquid fruit juice or water
4 apples, cut in eights, peel if desired
¼ cup sugar
1 dash cinnamon

Put liquid and 5 pieces of apple into blender. Cover and blend until smooth. Increase speed to frappe. Remove feeder cap and add remaining apples a few at a time.

Add sugar and cinnamon. Cook until creamy.

PEANUT BUTTER TREAT

½ cup butter
½ cup peanut butter
1 cup sugar
1 cup brown sugar
2 eggs
½ cup milk
1 tsp. vanilla
2 cups flour, sifted
1 tsp. baking soda
½ tsp. salt
2 cups oats
½ cup semi-sweet chocolate chips
½ cup raisins

Beat butter, peanut butter, sugars, and eggs. Add all other ingredients mixing well.

Drop 1 teaspoon size cookie dough unto ungreased cookie sheet. Bake 350° for 10-12 minutes.

FRUIT SHAKE

In blender mix until frothy:

Mango flavored orange juice
¼ mango or 1 peach, sliced or blueberries
6 ice cubes

BANANA MILK SHAKE

In blender mix until frothy:

1 glass milk
1 banana
1 peach (optional)
6 ice cubes

FRENCH BANANA PANCAKES

Pancakes:
1 cup flour
½ cup confection sugar
1 cup milk
2 eggs
3 tablespoons butter, melted
1 teaspoon vanilla extract
¼ teaspoon salt

Filling:
¼ cup butter
¼ cup packed brown sugar
¼ tsp. cinnamon
¼ teaspoon nutmeg
¼ cup light cream
5 or 6 firm bananas, halved lengthwise

Sift flour and confection sugar into a mixing bowl. Add milk, eggs, butter, vanilla and salt; beat until smooth.

Heat a lightly greased skillet; add about 3 tablespoons batter, spreading to almost bottom of skillet. Cook until lightly browned; turn and brown the other side. Remove to a wire rack. Repeat with remaining batter.

For filling, melt butter in a large skillet. Stir in brown sugar, cinnamon and nutmeg. Stir in cream and cook until slightly thickened.

Add half the bananas at a time to skillet, heat for 2-3 minutes, spooning sauce over them. Remove from heat.

Roll a pancake around each banana and place on serving platter.

RECIPE INDEX

JEAN N. PETRANTO

SOUPS

Bean with Tomatoes & Rice, 12
Best Onion, 9
Cabbage Minestra, 11
Cauliflower Soup, 8
Cream of Tomato, 13
Fresh Broccoli, 11
Lentil, 10
Minestrone, 7
Potato Corn Chowder, 14
Tomato & Carrot, 13
Vegetable Chowder, 14
Zucchini Minestra, 7

PASTA

Baked Ziti in Red Pepper Sauce, 26
Beef & Spinach Manicotti, 19
Chick Peas & Pasta, 18
Company Rice, 27
Fettuccine Carbonara, 21
Garlic & Oil Sauce, 17
Greens over Pasta, 26
Light Gnocchi, 17
Marinara Sauce, 25
Meatballs, 25
Mild Meatball Sauce, 24
Pork Rib and Sausage Sauce, 23
Red Clam Sauce, 22
Red Pepper Sauce, 23
Stuffed Shells or Manicotti, 19
White Clam Sauce, 21

VEGETABLES

Artichokes French, 32
Baked Cabbage, 33
Escarole & Beans, 33
Italian Green Bean Stew, 34
Italian Tomato Salad, 35
Mushroom Spinach Swirls, 31
One Pan Veggie Ratatouille, 35

MAIN DISHES

Blackened Catfish, 41
Braciole Beef Roll Up, 43
Braciola, 44
Chicken Thighs Treat, 49
Corned Beef & Cabbage, 45
Delicious Chunky Chili, 48
Easy Deep Elegant Brown Stew, 46
Easy Breakfast Menu, 49
Eggplant Parmesan, 42
Lunch Menu, 50
Meat Loaf Supreme, 45
Pepper Tripe Pot, 47
Special Seafood Fra Diavolo, 39
Salmon with Cheese Sauce, 40
Veal French, 47

DESSERTS

Cookies...
Chewy Chocolate Chip, 60
Chocolate Nutty, 59
Coconut Macaroon, 61
Coconut Sour Cream, 61
Cucidati (Italian Fig), 55
Delicious Date, 57

Holiday Fruit, 59
Jean's Italian Cookies, 53
Meatball, 58
Orange Drop, 54
Pfeffernusse, 57

Pies...
Apricot Cheese, 63
Chocolate Cheese, 65
Creamy Banana, 68
Custard, 66
Helpful Hints for Pie Crust, 57
Orange Velvet, 65
Peach, 67
Pear Pie, 64
Peanut Butter, 67
Raspberry or Cherry, 64
Sure Proof Pie Crust, 62

Cakes...
Apple, 73
Apple Spice, 73
Boston Cream, 70
Hummingbird, 69
Perfect Chocolate, 71
Ultimate Carrot, 77

More Sweets...
Apple Crisp, 76
Banana Milkshake, 87
Banana Squares, 78
Chocolate Sauce, 71
Chocolate Swirl Cheesecake with Raspberry Topping, 75
Cream Puff Pastry, 81
Freezer Buns, 83
Fresh Applesauce, 86
French Banana Pancakes, 88
Fruit Cobbler, 77
Fruit Shake, 87
Layered Banana Pudding, 82

Orange Cranberry Muffins, 83
Peanut Butter Treat, 86
Pineapple Cheesecake, 80
Quick Cinnamon Rolls, 85
Raspberry Cheese Squares, 79
Sweet Chocolate Glaze, 72

At the End of the Day

At the end of the day when I'm alone
At the end of the day on my way home
I think of the hurts & feel so sad
Then I think of the good & I'm glad
At the end of the day my family awaits
With love & a meal – then we say grace
At the end of the day we get on our knees
Help us tomorrow Lord
Thank you for today
Watch and protect us along the way
I love you Lord & will always pray
Until we meet in heaven someday

By J.N.P.

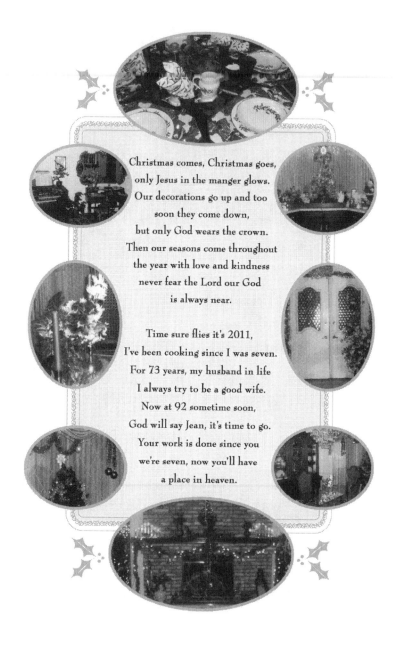

Christmas comes, Christmas goes,
only Jesus in the manger glows.
Our decorations go up and too
soon they come down,
but only God wears the crown.
Then our seasons come throughout
the year with love and kindness
never fear the Lord our God
is always near.

Time sure flies it's 2011,
I've been cooking since I was seven.
For 73 years, my husband in life
I always try to be a good wife.
Now at 92 sometime soon,
God will say Jean, it's time to go.
Your work is done since you
we're seven, now you'll have
a place in heaven.

AUTHOR JEAN N. PETRANTO

1988—our own 50th
wedding anniversary
celebration

Made in the USA
Charleston, SC
24 June 2013